PIANO REPERTOIRE
MASTERPIECES WITH FLAIR!
Book 1

Compiled and Edited by Jane Magrath

▼▼

CONTENTS

▲▲▲▲▲▲▲▲▲▲▲▲▲▲

▼▼▼▼▼▼▼▼▼▼▼▼▼▼▼

This book is dedicated to
Julie Sondag.
Jane Magrath

Preface

The pieces found in this anthology should be played *With Flair!* Included are both familiar and less familiar pieces, all of which require a strong spirit and a decisive interpretation. They are pieces that should motivate and inspire the performer. Not all are fast pieces. Various composi-

tional styles are represented with an intentionally large assemblage of literature from the Romantic period. It is the Romantic period literature that is still little known and underrepresented in today's teaching collections.

All works are original compositions presented in their original versions and are based on primary editions when possible. Editing has been kept to a minimum so that the essence of the composer's original text stands out. Most fingerings are editorial as are dynamic indications in the Baroque and, sparingly, in the Classical selections. All suggestions strive to steer the performer in the direction of the most authoritative and stylistically appropriate performance possible.

Students capable of playing standard classical literature from *Masterwork Classics*, Books 3–5 (easiest pieces by Haydn and Mozart, easiest works from the *Anna Magdalena Bach Notebook*, and Gurlitt's *Album for the Young*, Op. 140) may work from this volume. A suggested teaching order is provided only as a guide to assigning repertoire in this collection. The performer may also enjoy investigating literature in this book's companion volume, *Piano Repertoire … Melodious Masterpieces*, Book 1, also published by Alfred Publishing Company.

The editor extends warm thanks and appreciation to Morty and Iris Manus for their insight, help, encouragement and continuous support. Appreciation is extended also to David Smooke for his perception and careful work.

▼▼▼

Practice Notes

▲▲▲▲▲▲▲▲▲▲▲▲▲▲

BACH

The performer should feel the tension build through each phrase as the harmonies progress. Strive to match the intensity of tone from one note to another within a phrase.

BEETHOVEN

Both of these dances are energetic and boisterous, reflecting good nature and earthiness. With thick textures such as these, a primary consideration should always be to maintain fine voicing of the melody above the accompanying voices. Strong contrast in dynamic levels is essential.

CLARKE

A fanfarelike work, *King William's March* needs a steady sense of rhythm throughout. Play the quarter notes slightly detached.

DIABELLI

This sprightly work calls for buoyant staccato notes and a steady tempo, and should be played in a lighthearted and cheerful manner. Strive to play the theme beginning in measure 9 with a different character from that in the opening measures.

DUNCOMBE

This stately piece needs a steady rhythm throughout to help portray the mood of a trumpet announcement for an important event. Maintain a loose wrist while playing the thirds beginning in measure 9.

HAYDN

This playful piece is filled with surprise and humor, as in the repetition of the melody an octave higher in measure 39. Exaggerate contrasts in dynamic levels.

Play these dances with a feeling of one pulse per measure. Chords in the left hand should never drown out the melody.

ELLMENREICH

The repetition in the left hand, and later in the right hand of the B section, probably represents the regularity of a spinning wheel. Avoid rushing to the syncopated beats throughout. This piece has a 2/4 time signature. Be sure to feel two beats per measure, not four.

GURLITT

This passionate piece calls for a strongly defined bass that sings out above the repeated-note accompaniment in the right hand. Strive for rounded phrases and a singing tone.

Pay special attention to the articulation from the earliest stages of learning *The Fair*. Notice how much repetition occurs in this piece, making for ease in study.

Throughout, listen for the repeated figures and the continuous eighth notes representing the repetitive motions heard at a mill. The staccatos should be exact and quite short. The work is in three sections.

The piece capitalizes on repetition so that after learning several ideas well, the student will find the piece to be quite manageable. The work represents the *Sturm und Drang* or *Storm and Stress* movement, a time during the Romantic period when artistic creations were filled with emotion, passion and drama.

▼▼▼

HELLER

This lively work by Heller calls for smoothly alternating between the right and left hands. The *meno mosso* sections should be evenly incorporated into the texture without any sudden changes in tempo. The coda beginning in measure 73 needs strong energy and total evenness.

OESTEN

Throughout this piece, the melody appears in the right hand while the left hand features repeated chords in the accompaniment. Strive for a strong rhythmic feeling. The accented notes are also usually staccato notes. Do not make the accents too heavy.

REINHOLD

This robust work calls for a spirited performance and a rich, rounded tone. The double-note passages here need to be played so that the melody in the top voice projects above the accompaniment. Strive for a true finger legato as much as possible in measures 11–18 as well as in the right hand of the main theme.

Strive for a flexible tempo with some rubato to portray the flair and festivity of a Hungarian dance. The changing of fingers on a single note, as in measures 1 and 2, allows the strongest fingers to be used, thus aiding in achieving clarity. Strive for absolute accuracy in fingering from the earliest stages of learning this work. Even with the flexibility of tempo, the passagework must maintain clarity.

SCHUMANN

The feeling of having worked hard and now being ready for rest and relaxation is reflected in this robust and cheerful piece. Playing so the accompaniment (usually in the right hand) sounds beneath the melody is the main challenge of this piece.

Again, skillful voicing is essential in this lively work in which the staccato notes and disjunct melody perhaps represent the jumping and galloping of a horse and rider.

BARTÓK

Play Song is based on a Hungarian folk tune. Choose a sufficiently moderate tempo at the beginning so that the *più mosso* section (measures 19–32) can be faster without being too difficult. Work for clear voicing of the melody over the accompaniment.

Note that the phrase lengths within this piece increase. There are three phrases in the entire work and they are, consecutively, 2 measures, 3 measures and 5 measures long. Although *Rhythmic Dance* is written in four voices, often one or two of the voices remain static. The entire piece is built upon the rhythmic motive that appears in the first measure of the piece.

GRETCHANINOFF

This zestful work calls for a strong rhythmic sense and a bold interpretation.

▼▼

KABALEVSKY

The staccato passages and rapid finger passages give this work its cheerful and dazzling feeling. The hands must be absolutely synchronized.

No finer study in the playing of chord inversions at this level can be found. Avoid rushing the last two eighth notes of each measure. Strive for long phrases.

MAYKAPAR

The image of a butterfly flitting around is clearly depicted in this programmatic work. To facilitate the learning process, discover the patterns in this work.

In the Garden is a work built on repeated rhythmic patterns, repeated tones and sparkling staccatos. It is necessary to clearly project the top voice. Avoid rushing the eighth-note pulse within each measure.

The use of the very high register of the piano helps portray the sound of a music box. The repetition of the theme with variation in the accompaniment in measure 16 makes this piece easy to learn.

This work is a study in chords and inversions. The pedal is used primarily to accent rather than to sustain tones. This work is most effective if played in eight-measure phrase lengths.

*This page has been left blank in order to eliminate
an awkward page turn.*

Trumpet Tune

William Duncombe
(1690–1769)

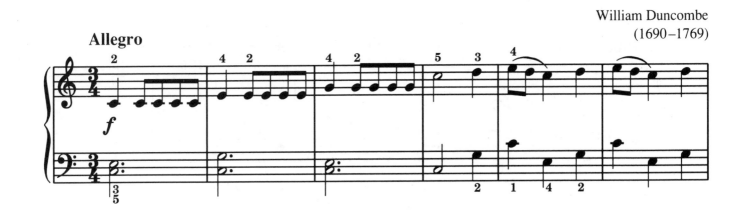

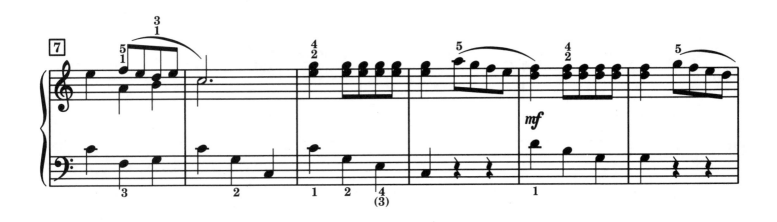

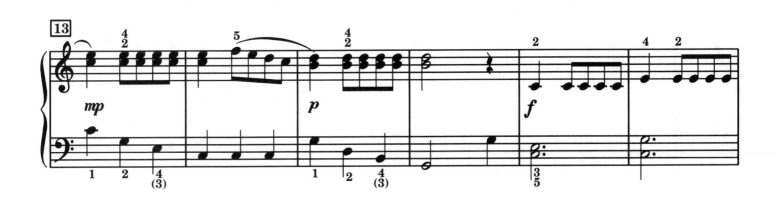

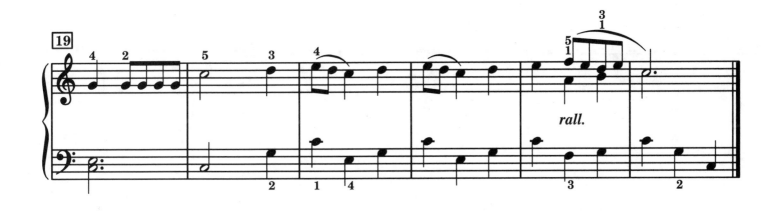

King William's March

Jeremiah Clarke
(1673–1707)

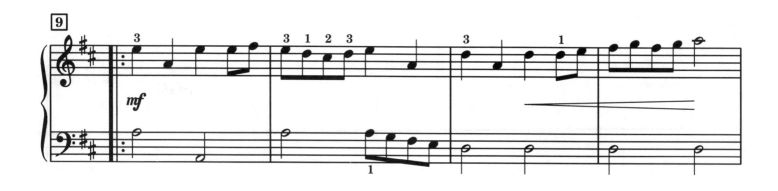

Short Prelude in C Major

Johann Sebastian Bach (1685–1750)

BWV 939

Bagatelle

from *10 Short Pieces*

Anton Diabelli
(1781–1858)

German Dance in D Major

Franz Joseph Haydn (1732–1809)
Hob. IX:22/2

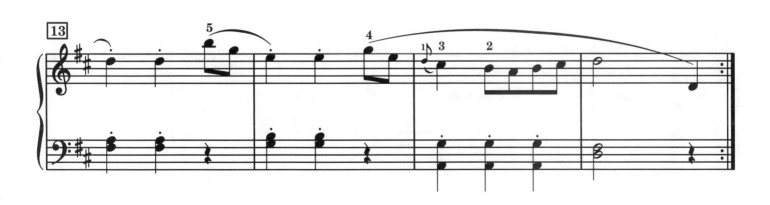

Allegro scherzando in F Major

Franz Joseph Haydn (1732–1809)
Hob. III:75/4

German Dance in E Major

Franz Joseph Haydn (1732–1809)
Hob. IX:22/9

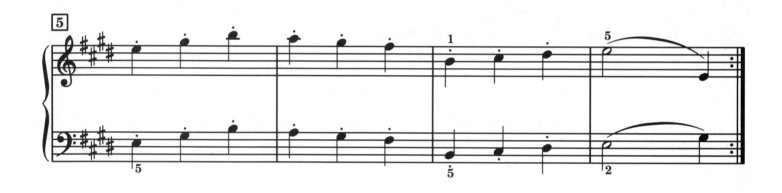

Country Dance in D Major

Ludwig van Beethoven (1770–1827)
WoO 15, No. 1

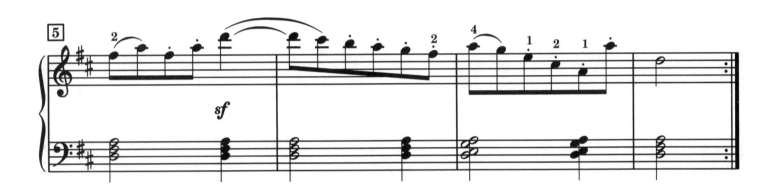

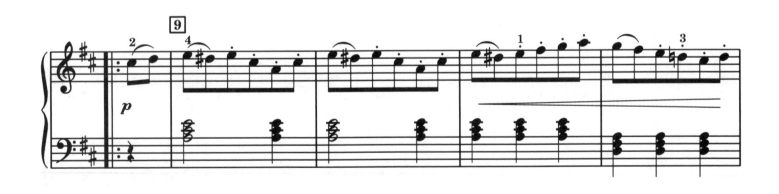

Country Dance in D Major

Ludwig van Beethoven (1770–1827)

WoO 11, No. 7

The Happy Farmer

Robert Schumann (1810–1856)
Op. 68, No. 10

(Brisk and cheerful)
Frisch und munter

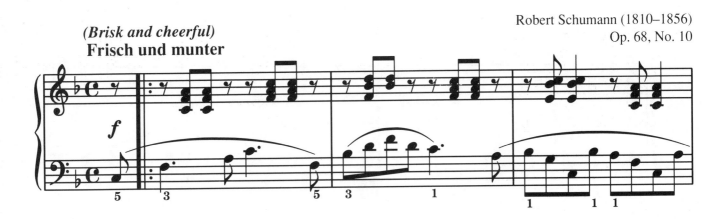

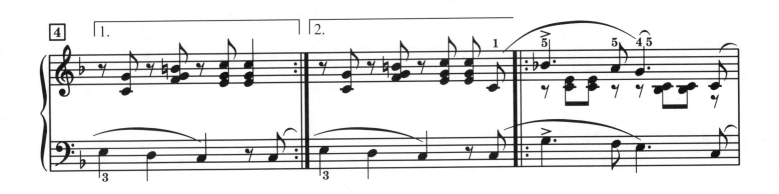

The Wild Rider

Robert Schumann (1810–1850)
Op. 68, No. 8

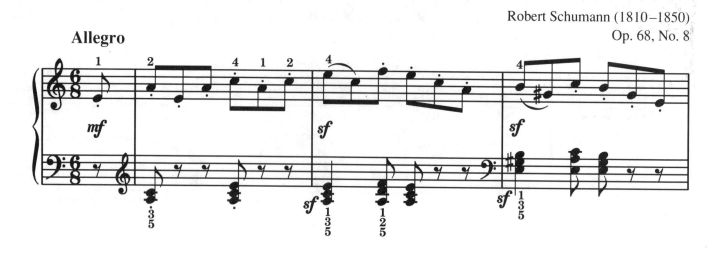

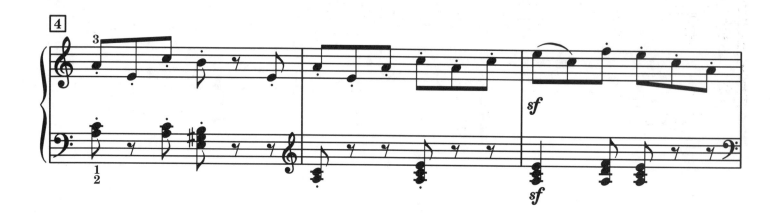

Spanish Dance

Theodore Oesten (1813–1870)
Op. 61, No. 10

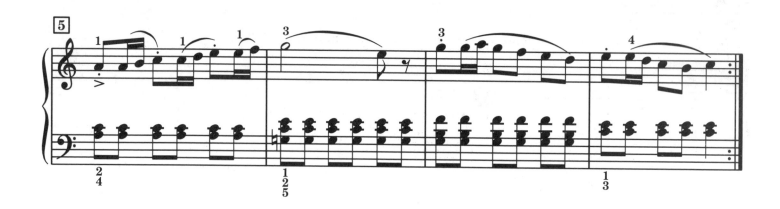

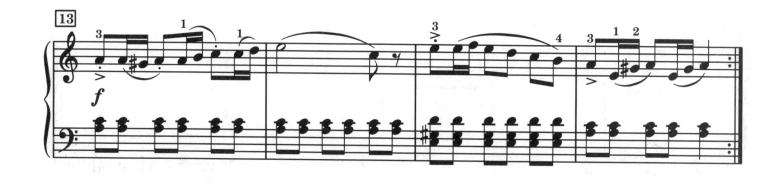

The Mill

Cornelius Gurlitt (1820–1901)
Op. 117, No. 33

Moderato

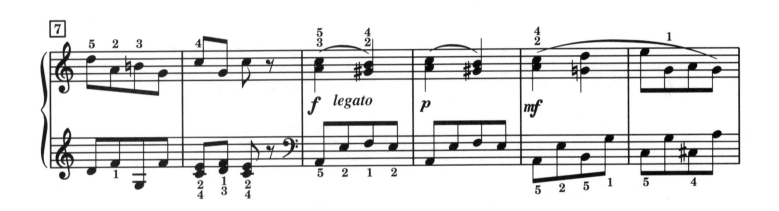

The Fair

Cornelius Gurlitt (1820–1901)
Op. 101, No. 8

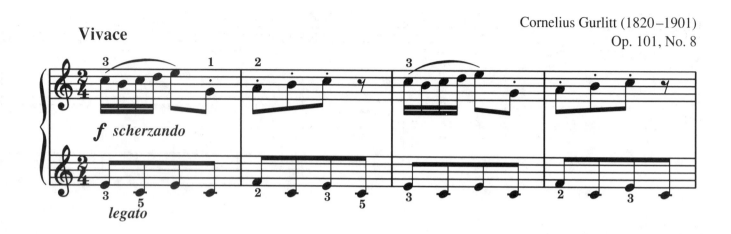

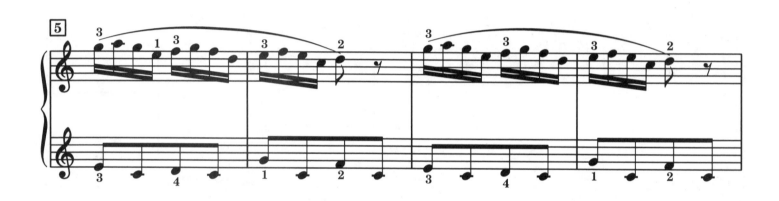

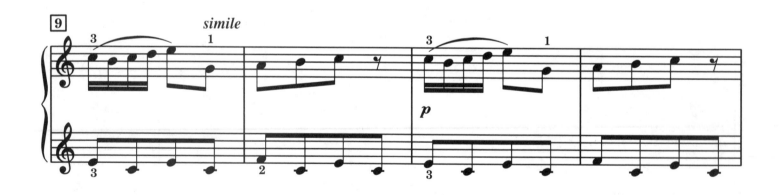

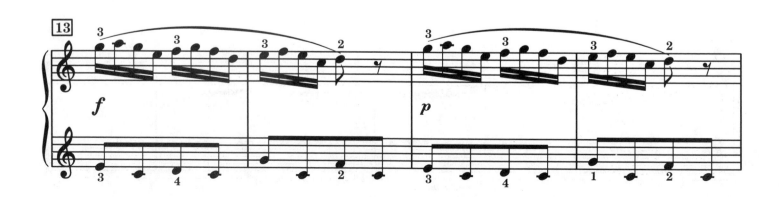

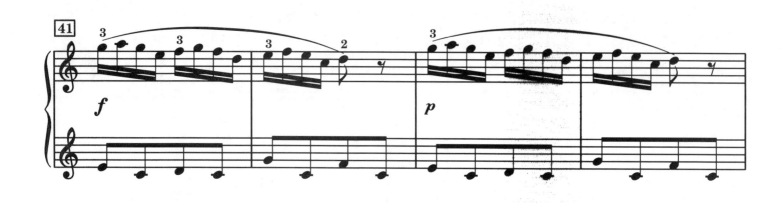

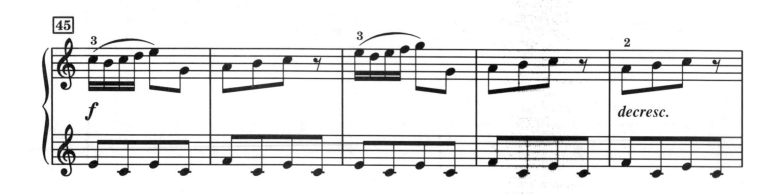

Allegro non troppo

Cornelius Gurlitt (1820–1901)
Op. 82, No. 65

Allegro non troppo

Storm and Stress

Cornelius Gurlitt (1820–1901)
Op. 140, No. 20

Gypsy Song

Hugo Reinhold (1854–1935)
Op. 39, No. 13

Hungarian Dance

Hugo Reinhold (1854–1935)
Op. 39, No. 9

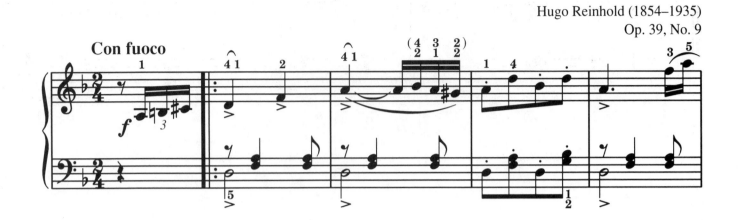

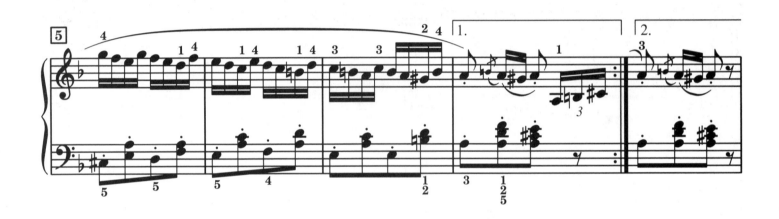

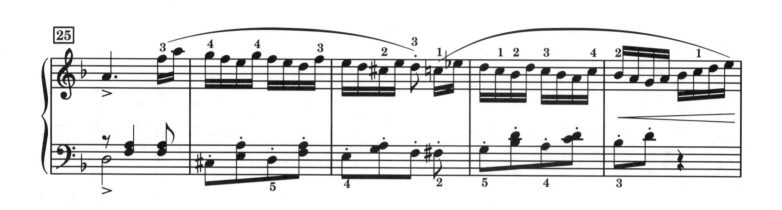

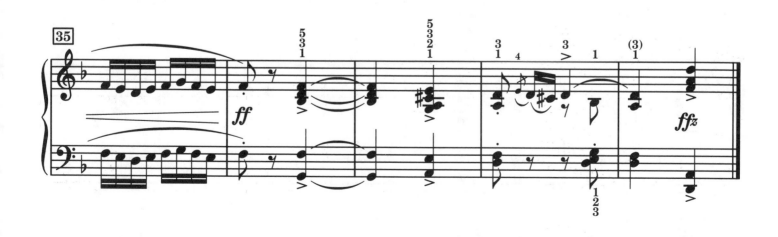

Spinning Song

Albert Ellmenreich (1816–1905)
Op. 14, No. 4

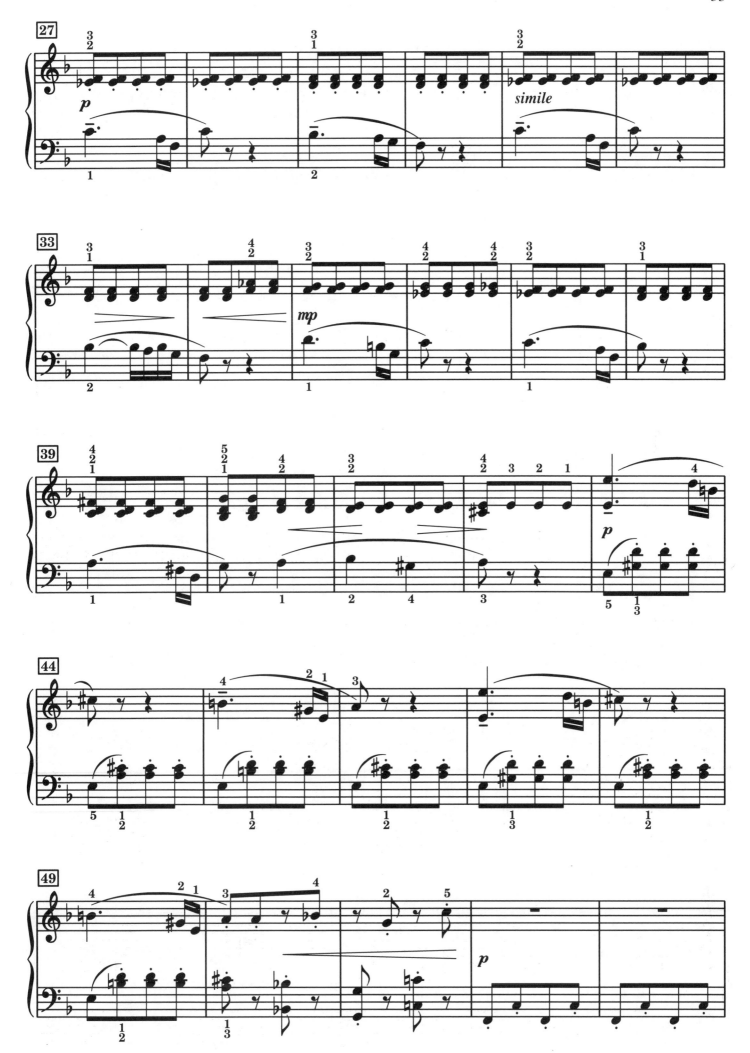

The Avalanche

Stephen Heller (1813–1888)
Op. 45, No. 2

Prelude No. 1

Samuel Maykapar
(1867–1938)

In the Garden

Samuel Maykapar (1867–1938)
Op. 28, No. 1

The Butterfly

Samuel Maykapar (1867–1938)
Op. 28, No. 12

Allegro grazioso e volante

The Music Box

Allegro giocoso

Both hands 8va throughout

Samuel Maykapar (1867–1938)
Op. 28, No. 13

Holidays

Alexander Gretchaninoff (1864–1956)
Op. 119, No. 17

Allegro non troppo

A Merry Tune

Dmitri Kabalevsky (1904–1987)
Op. 89, No. 26

Toccatina

Dmitri Kabalevsky (1904–1987)
Op. 27, No. 12

* For an alternate fingering, use $\frac{5}{2}$ on all right-hand chords.

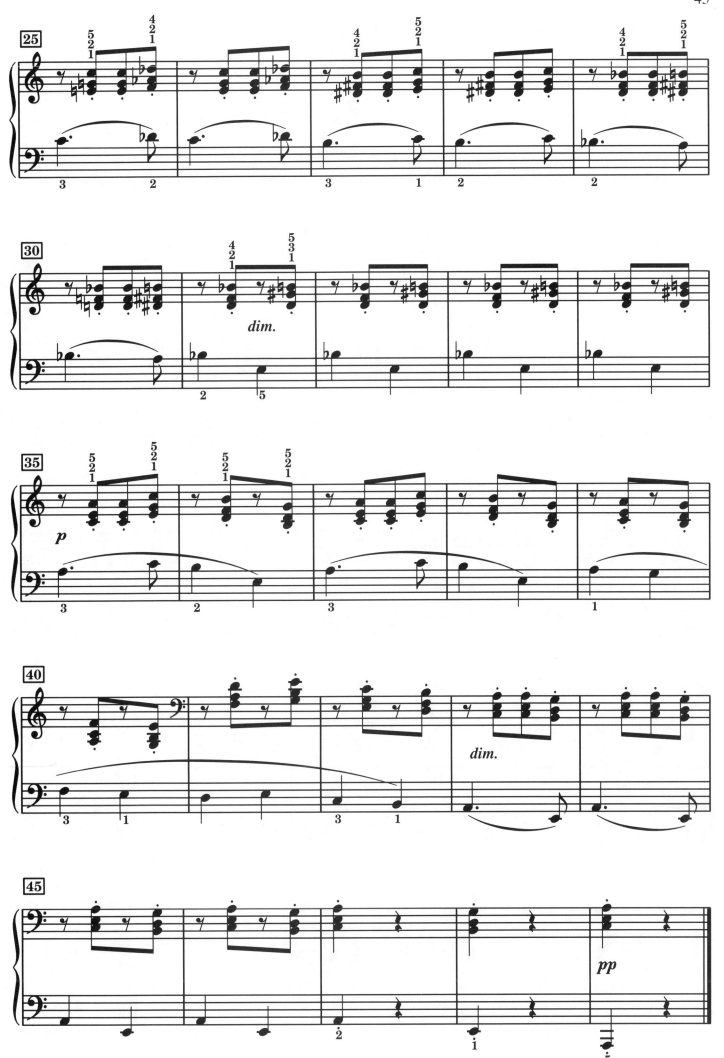

Play Song

Béla Bartók
(1881–1945)

Rhythmic Dance

Béla Bartók
(1881–1945)

Allegro deciso